A Travel Companion to the

Wineries of the Pacific Northwest

*featuring the Pinot Noirs
of Oregon's Willamette Valley*

By D. L. Tadevich

p+ PUBLISHING-PLUS

Publishing Plus:
A division of Insurance Publishing Plus Corporation
11690 Technology Drive
Carmel IN 46032 USA

www.ewinetravelbooks.com

Acknowledgements

My special thanks go to Walter J. Gdowski, chairman and CEO of Insurance Publishing Plus. To Don Marsh, Jr., for believing in my travel guide-books and providing access on his supermarket shelves. And to my two daughters, Melanie and Isabella.

I would also like to thank my mother, Diane Allen for her time and steadfast energy that she devoted to assisting in the preliminary research for each winery, her organizational skills, and most importantly her perseverance in making this book a reality.

A Travel Companion to the
Wineries of the Pacific Northwest
featuring the Pinot Noirs of Oregon's Willamette Valley

By D. L. Tadevich

www.ewinetravelbooks.com

Writer
D. L. Tadevich

Project Editor
Heidi Newman, Mark My Word!
Indianapolis, Indiana

Designer
Karen J. Kennedy, Major Productions, Inc.
Indianapolis, Indiana

Researcher
Georgianna Quinn, Carmel Indiana

Photography and Grape and Winery Art
Cheryl Rogers Designs
Scappoose, Oregon

First Edition, 2002

Copyright © 2002 D. L. Tadevich.
All rights reserved

PPUBLISHING–PLUS

Publishing Plus:
A division of Insurance Publishing Plus Corporation
11690 Technology Drive
Carmel IN 46032 USA
(800) 211-3257

ISBN 0-9704154-2-7

Printed in Canada

Table of Contents

D. L. Tadevich

Author of A Travel Companion to Lake Erie Wineries, Wineries of Michigan *and* Wineries of Indiana. *Her books are distributed in major national book-stores, as well as online through Amazon.com and ewinetravelbooks.com. She founded Tadevich & Associates in New York City, a company specializing in photo journalism books and high-tech permanent historical exhibits. Debra has received a Clarion award for popular history writing, and her marketing company was a collaberating finalist for the New York Festivals' International Television Advertising Award. She lives in Indianapolis with her two daughters.*

Cheryl Rogers, photographer and fine artist

She specializes in producing hand-painted, mixed-media fine art. Cheryl's limited edition prints and exclusive line of artwork can be found at the International Pinot Noir Celebration, in select wineries, wine shops, specialty shops and galleries. Cheryl, her husband, Neil, and their chocolate Lab, Radar, live on a hilltop in Scappoose, Oregon.

Pinot Noir

Pinot
Gris

Cheryl Rogers

Introduction

In the last two decades Oregon has gained recognition for its exquisite Pinot noirs which are often compared to those produced in the renowned Burgundy region of France. Because Oregon and Burgundy share the same northern latitude and similar grape-growing conditions, both are ideal for crafting world-class wines.

The Willamette Valley is the best-known wine region in Oregon, and this guidebook includes a sampling of  wineries within this lush valley. We focused on wineries geographically suited for a relaxed and varied tour, and those with tasting room ambiance, welcoming hospitality—and most importantly, fabulous wines. You will find many vintages to sample, however most vintners agree that the best harvests were in 1998, 1999, 2000 and 2001.

Pinot Noir

Good Pinot noir wine is silky and rich with fruit fragrance. Starting with vines planted in the ideal locales and soils, and incorporating the Burgundy style of winemaking, Oregon produces some of the best Pinot noir in the U.S.

Oregon Pinot noirs are generally full of the soft flavors of red cherries, raspberries, and strawberries. However, the darker the shade of the Pinot, the more you will taste an intense black fruit flavor. Many of the wineries ferment and age the Pinot noirs in oak—usually French oak.

Pinot noir is a food-friendly wine. Drink it with fish and fowl, and meats such as veal or pork. Or try a Pinot with spicy food, such as Indian curries or tandoori chicken, or chili-laced Thai cuisine.

If you are a chocolate junkie, enjoy a glass—or if you are depressed, a bottle—with a box of chocolates. Some of the wineries even sell their own brand of chocolates made with Pinot noir. Double decadence!

Pinot Gris (Pinot Grigio is the Italian moniker)

Oregon Pinot gris is made in the typical Alsace style with peachy and tropical fruit flavors, but without the buttery and oak overtones. This wine is aromatic and intense. Pinot gris is usually semi-dry and crisp. Drink Pinot gris with lean fish, shellfish, or smoked turkey or ham.

Have fun touring and don't forget to designate a driver if you are going to spend the day wine tasting. Or, follow the lead of the connoisseurs and simply taste and cracker, or spit it out.

History

The Oregon wine industry began in 1959 with a few pioneers seeking a new area to grow premium grapes outside of California. There were only a handful of vintners who followed this path. The first was Richard Sommer of Hillcrest Winery who put down stakes in 1961 in the southern part of the state. Just four years later, David Lett followed Sommer to Oregon and planted north in the Willamette Valley.

The early vintners had to fight a very popular view—that premium wine grapes could not grow in cold climates. However, many states, including Oregon, have proven this to be only a theory and not a reality. Currently the major varieties produced in Oregon are Pinot noir, Pinot blanc, Pinot gris, Cabernet Sauvignon, Chardonnay, Gewürztraminer, Merlot, Müller-Thurgau, Sauvignon blanc, Semillon, Syrah (called Shiraz, Down Under) and Zinfandel.

By 1990 Oregon had 71 wineries. Today there are more than 190 and the list grows each year. Today Oregon ranks 2nd in the nation for the number of wineries and 4th for production output, and has more than 10,000 acres of wine grapes. The Willamette Valley is the most famous of the designated appellation areas, with the Rogue and Umpqua Valley regions demonstrating production increases every year. These appelation regions are joined by Walla Walla, Columbia Valley, and the newest, Applegate Valley.

Oregon has some of the strictest of the nation's laws governing the wine industry. Appellations are mandatory for labeled varietal wines—which must be produced from fruit grown in the state's region of origin. Oregon wines must also contain a minimum of 90% of the variety stated on the label, with the exception of Cabernet Sauvignon (minimum 75% required).

The Willamette Valley stretches from Portland in the north to Eugene in the south. The valley sports more than 100 wineries meandering through luscious farmland and overlooking tranquil hillsides and sparkling rivers.

The North Willamette Valley's marine climate has terrain which subdues any weather extremes. The winters are cold and wet allowing the premier grapes a necessary dormant season followed by dry summers. There are over 6,000 acres of wine grapes gracing the volcanic hillsides. The vineyards are planted in soils that are naturally well drained, and most slopes face the south for full sunlight exposure. During harvest season, North Willamette can receive up to 40 inches of rain between November and April which makes picking the grapes a day-by-day adventure.

The South Willamette region is warmer and therefore more dense with wineries. The soil is clay and loamy, nurturing nearly 1,000 acres of vineyards. The most popular wine grapes grown in the Willamette Valley are the red and white Pinots, Chardonnay and Riesling, whose vines are nourished by approximately 35 inches of rain each autumn.

Most of Oregon's wineries are small and yield modest wine production, so a vintage can sell out pretty quickly. The most produced wine in the Willamette Valley is Pinot noir (and the second most produced wine is now Chardonnay). Oregon's "International Pinot Noir Celebration"(INPC), is an internationally acclaimed festival and the Oregon wineries compete furiously to be among the select few featured. The tickets are expensive—around $800 per person for the three-day festival of wine and excellent food.

GLOSSARY OF WINE TERMS

Acidic A wine that is unbalanced, making it sharp, sour or tart.

Aftertaste (or Finish) The lingering impression of the taste of the wine after swallowing. It may be short, lingering, long, clean, dirty, or have other pleasant or unpleasant features.

Balance Refers to the proportion or harmony of the various elements of wine taste such as fruit, oak, acid, sweetness and tannin.

Body The tactile impression of fullness on the palate due to alcohol, glycerin, residual sugar and extract.

Bouquet The scents or odors that originate from aging. Bouquet emerges as the wine matures.

Breathing Allowing a wine to stand open–preferably in a decanter–for an hour or two before being consumed. This may have the effect of dissipating off-odors and mellowing or enhancing flavors.

Complex(ity) A wine containing many different aromas, bouquets and flavors, producing a pleasing harmony.

Fermentation The process of converting sugars to ethyl alcohol by yeasts in the juice of fruits or vegetables. Carbon dioxide is a by-product of this process. See Malolactic Fermentation.

Fruity The fragrance or flavor of young wines that are especially aromatic; also the fragrance of wines that smell decisively of the grape variety from which they were made. Sometimes confused with sweetness, fruity wines can also be dry.

Full-bodied The feel in the mouth when a wine is high in alcohol and/or extract.

Malolactic Fermentation A secondary fermentation caused by bacteria that converts malic acid (a sharp acid) to lactic acid (a softer acid). This is done to soften a wine's acidity. This does not occur in all wines.

Methode Champenoise The traditional method of producing sparkling wine by causing a secondary fermentation in the bottle instead of in a tank. This produces the highest quality sparkling wines.

Microclimate Often used to refer to the vineyard site and surrounding area. The correct term is mesoclimate. True microclimate is the zone within and immediately surrounding an individual vine.

Phylloxera A vine-killing root louse that has infected the world's vineyards necessitating that nearly all vines be grafted to resistant hybrid rootstocks. Native American varieties and many of their hybrids are immune.

Sparkling Wines The correct name for wines that contain carbon dioxide bubbles. Normally this occurs by a secondary fermentation in a closed container. Not all of these wines are Champagne, a name used only for sparkling wines from that region in France. See Methode Champenoise

Sur-Lie Refers to leaving the newly fermented wine with the lees (sediments) in order to create more body and complexity.

Tannin A bitter, astringent acid derived from skins, seeds and wooden barrels that causes a puckery sensation in the mouth and throat. Tannin dissipates with time, thus the recommendation that red wines need to age.

Unbalanced A wine lacking harmony among its acid, sugar, fruit, oak or tannin components, usually with one dominating the others.

Varietal Refers to a wine named after the grape variety from which it was principally made; and to wines that exemplify to a high degree the typical attributes of a variety.

Viticultural Area (Appellation/Denomination) A delimited region where common geographical or climatic attributes contribute to a unique and definable character in the wine. American Viticultural Areas (AVAs) are approved by the federal government. In Europe, appellations and denominations may also mandate grape varieties, ripeness levels, crop levels and more.

How Wine Is Made

This section is intended to be a very brief overview.

Winemaking

The winemaker is the person who turns grapes into wine. **Enology** is the science of wines and winemaking. An **enologist** has earned a degree in the science of winemaking. **Viticulture** is the science, or art, of grape growing. **Vinification** is the process of turning grape juice into wine.

Grape Harvest

Harvest time can vary, beginning as early as late August and, sometimes extending into November. Harvest is a winery's busiest season, and those wineries that cultivate their own grapes usually work around the clock. Grapes can be picked by machine or by hand, and are then transported to the winery as quickly as possible. Sulphur dioxide will be added when the grapes are crushed to prevent spoilage and to kill wild yeasts.

Red Wine

The red grapes are not harvested until they are as ripe as possible. The fruit's ripeness is an important factor in the quality of red wine. It is the skin of the red-wine grapes that gives the wine its color, tannin and the many fruit flavors that red wine lovers enjoy. Once the grapes have been picked, the under-ripe and rotten ones are discarded. The grapes are then lightly crushed into a thick mush, called **'must,'** and all stalks are removed. The must is then transferred into stainless steel tanks or oak barrels. The grapes may sit in their juices and soften for hours or even days before the winemaker begins the **fermentation**. This process is called **'cold soaking'**.

Fermentation occurs when yeast cells convert the sugar in the juice into alcohol. Using cultured yeast, the winemaker sets the temperature in the tanks at 77-86 degrees Fahrenheit. Converting all of the sugar into alcohol usually takes less than two weeks.

Most red wines and some white wines go through a second **'malolactic'** fermentation in which the sharper malic acid is converted to lactic acid. The new wine may be left to sit on the skins for one to four weeks after the first fermentation. During this time, the color will redden and the **tannin** will soften. (Tannin is in the skin of the red grape and gives an astringent taste to the wine. This astringency is magnified if the wine is chilled when it is consumed— so most red wines are served at room temperature.)

Finally, the wine is drawn from the tank. The first wine is called the free-run, because it freely runs out of the tank. The remaining wine, which contains slightly more tannin, is squeezed out by a winepress. It is then mixed in with the free-run juice (in proportions chosen by the individual winemaker) in order to adjust the tannin level in the wine. The wine is clarified to rid it of solids and remove any cloudiness. Finally, the wine is placed in stainless steel tanks or oak barrels to age. When it reaches the determined maturation date, the wine is bottled.

How long should wine age? Some wine is sold immediately to the consumer. If the winery is producing a fine wine, it could sit for one year or more before distribution.

It is a misconception that wine, red or white, aged in oak is better than wine aged in stainless steel. This is a matter of individual taste. (Tastes associated with oak aging are nutmeg, vanilla, chocolate or smoke.)

White Wine

It is trickier for the winemaker to make a good white wine than to make a good red wine. The white grape skins are thin and, consequently, can rot faster or overcook in the sun. Because the fruit must be harvested at just the right time, it becomes a delicate balancing act between too soon and too late.

White grapes go to the pressing machines, and the grape juice is immediately separated from the skins and stems. (For Chardonnay and Gewürztraminer, the juice may be left in contact with the skins for a longer time.) The juice is now ready for fermentation, which takes place at a cooler temperature—50-70 degrees Fahrenheit.

The lower temperatures create a light, crisp wine. Yet, the warmer the temperature, the fuller the wine. The rest of the process is essentially the same as for red wines.

Rosé—or a more modern name—Blush Wine

Blush wines are made from red grapes, but with the same processing as white wines. The juice is allowed a very short period of contact, usually a few hours, with the skins before they're removed—giving blush its 'pink' color.

From Dry to Sweet

When all the sugar in the grapes has been converted to alcohol, the wine is said to be dry. However, there are ways of keeping some residual sugar. The winemaker can filter out the yeast whenever desired during the process. Sterilized unfermented juice may be added back at the end. The result is that any grape can be made to produce a wine as sweet or dry as desired.

Blending the Grapes

Many wines—both red and white—are blends of different grape varieties. Different wines can be fermented separately and then brought together later. The winemaker can blend different barrels of wine from the same grape variety, or wines from different vineyards, or even different regions, to create one kind of wine before bottling. Blending is an age-old tradition just about anywhere that you can find a winemaker.

Sparkling Wines

Traditional sparkling wines are made from a combination of red- and white-skinned grapes. The winemaking production method begins the same as with still wine—the grapes are pressed quickly and then fermented to create a dry wine. Red grapes are treated as they are for blush wines.

When grape juice ferments, carbon dioxide gas is released into the atmosphere. However, if the winemaker wants to produce sparkling wine, the carbon dioxide gas must be prevented from escaping. So the winemaker takes the wine, adds a controlled amount of sugar and yeast, and induces a second fermentation in a closed container.

The two methods that are used to make sparkling wines are the **Methode Champenoise**, a traditional method of second fermentation in the bottle, and the **Charmat** method, in which carbon dioxide gas is trapped in the tank and fermentation takes place there.

If the winemaker is using the Champenoise method to make the sparkling wine, the wine stays in the same bottle from the second fermentation until it is sold. The bottles are left untouched for months—or even years, for the higher quality sparkling wines. During this time, a slow process called autolysis takes place. The spent yeast cells come in contact with the wine in the bottle and are slowly destroyed by their own enzymes. The autolysis process is important to the taste factor. The longer the yeast is in contact with the wine, the more the flavor takes on the yeast characteristics.

There is another important factor in the length of time the sparkling wine is aged. In the second fermentation, the carbon dioxide is trapped. The longer the wine sits, the more the gas becomes incorporated into the wine, and the more slowly it is released from the wine in the glass.

There are still sediments left in the wine, so winemakers use a method called riddling, a gentle turning of the bottles by hand, to get the sediments to settle onto the cap and eventually pop out. The neck of the bottle is submerged in a solution with temperatures below freezing. The idea is to freeze the sediment resting upon the cap into an ice plug. Once frozen, the winemaker turns the bottle up and pops off the cap. The sediment, trapped in its ice cube, shoots out of the bottle. The bottle is then resealed with the champagne cork.

The entire Champenoise method is very time consuming and labor intensive and is reserved for the higher quality grape varieties. 🍷

How to Read a Wine Label

WILLAMETTE VALLEY
VINEYARDS

Oregon

98

1998

PINOT NOIR

the name of the winery

the 'vintage' or year
in which the grapes
were harvested.

the wine's appellation;
the federally approved
'American Viticultural
Area' where the grapes
were grown.

the name of the
grape variety.

Lange

2000

the name of the winery

Pinot Gris

YAMHILL VINEYARDS
RESERVE

Willamette Valley

ALC 13.0% BY VOLUME

the name of the wine. This name is the property of the winery and no one else can use it, thus the name is 'proprietary.'

indicates that the wine contains between 7% and 14% alcohol.

CAMERON

Willamette Valley

PINOT NOIR

PRODUCED AND BOTTLED BY
RON WINERY, DUNDEE, OREGON USA BY VO
ALCOHOL 13% BY VOLUME

1999

Chateau Lor

TINORE
ATE

HINMAN VINEYARDS

ILLAMETTE VALL

VINEYARDS

Oregon

199

PINOT

FRIES' FAM

Duck

2000

Gewürztramin

1996
Pinot Noir

TUALATIN ESTATE

LLAMETTE VALLEY

WILLAMETTE VALLEY
OREGON

13

rainbow

The Art of Wine Tasting

Visual

To really examine a wine, hold a glassful in the air against either light from a window, a white background, or a lamp. The color of the wine changes depending on the particular grape variety. Wines with deep color are usually fuller tasting. In a red wine, the purple color indicates a young wine and a red-brown indicates an older vintage. As for white wines, a young wine will be nearly colorless and an aged white wine will be a gold or deep gold color.

Smelling or Sniffing

Pour about one to two ounces of wine in your glass, hold it by the stem and swirl the wine to release the aromas. After you swirl, put your nose to the rim and deep into the glass, making the upper rim touch the bridge of your nose. You will smell fruity, spicy, or wood odors.

Tasting

When you are wine tasting, it is better to taste the white wines before the red wines, dry before sweet wines, and older vintages before young wines. Swish a mouthful of wine around so it touches all sides of your tongue and the roof of your mouth. If you are sampling a dry red wine, aerate it by imitating the motion of whistling backward to draw in air with the wine in your mouth. This helps release its full flavor and character.

Spitting

If you are touring many wineries, it is advisable to spit–and don't be shy about it. Wineries do not take offense at this and often have a bucket for you to spit in. If you are uncomfortable spitting, just take a sip and leave the rest. Then ask for just a taste of additional samples.

Storing

When storing wine, the cork must be kept moist. The bottle should be placed on its side or upside down. Wine should be kept in a room that is cool, 55-65 degrees Fahrenheit, and should not be exposed to heat or direct sunlight.

Serving

Before serving champagne or sparkling wine, it is good to chill it for three hours at 40 degrees Fahrenheit. White wines should chill for two hours at 45-50 degrees Fahrenheit. Red wine is served at room temperature, usually 60-65 degrees Fahrenheit, and should be opened to air for one hour before serving. Air softens the tannins and intensifies the bouquet.

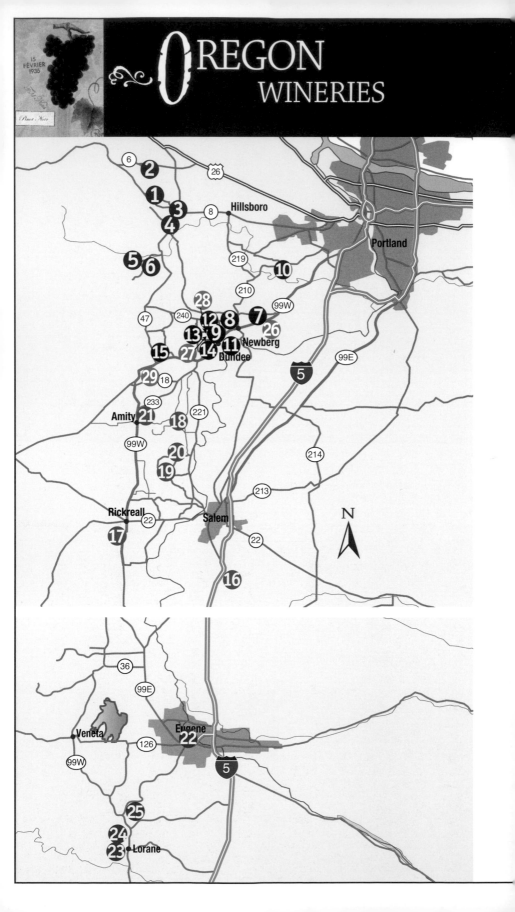

Name	Map Code	Full Service Restaurant	Winery Tours	Picnicking	Gift Shop	Tours by Appointment	Vineyard
David Hill Vineyard & Winery	1		●	●	●		●
ualatin Estate	2		●	●	●		●
Momokawa Saké/SakéOne	3		●	●	●		●
Montinore Estate	4		●	●	●		●
Elk Cove Vineyards	5		●	●	●		●
Kramer Vineyards	6		●	●	●		●
Rex Hill Vineyards	7		●	●	●		●
Duck Pond Cellars	8		●	●	●		●
Dundee Springs Winery, Perry Bower Vineyard	9		●	●	●		●
Ponzi Vineyards	10	●	●	●	●		●
Argyle Winery	11		●	●	●		●
Winery	12		●	●	●		●
Erath Vineyards	13		●	●	●		●
Sokol Blosser Winery	14		●	●	●		●
Chateau Benoit	15		●	●	●		●
Willamette Valley Vineyards	16		●	●	●		●
Eola Hills Wine Cellars	17		●	●	●		●
Bethel Heights Vineyard	18		●	●	●		●
Cristom	19		●	●	●		●
Witness Tree Vineyard	20		●	●	●		●
Amity Vineyards	21		●	●	●		●
Eugene Wine Cellars	22		●	●	●		●
Chateau Lorane	23		●	●	●		●
King Estate	24		●	●	●		●
Hinman Vineyards/Silvan Ridge	25		●	●	●		●
Chehalem	26					●	●
Cameron Winery	27					●	●
Domaine Drouhin	28					●	●
Westrey Wine Company	29					●	●

TOUR 1

This tour is in Washington County. The wineries are more scattered than those farther south. However, this makes the tour more exciting and adventuresome. You will wind around rolling hills, cross over rivers, and pass through valleys with breathtaking scenery.

Our tour begins in Forest Grove where the vineyards sit at the western margin looking toward the Chehalem Mountains and the Taulatin River. The wineries are quaint and have a lot of personality. The proprietors are usually around and fun to talk with, particularly if you know about the region's wines.

Have fun, drive safely, and enjoy your wine tasting adventure.

This tour takes approximately six hours.

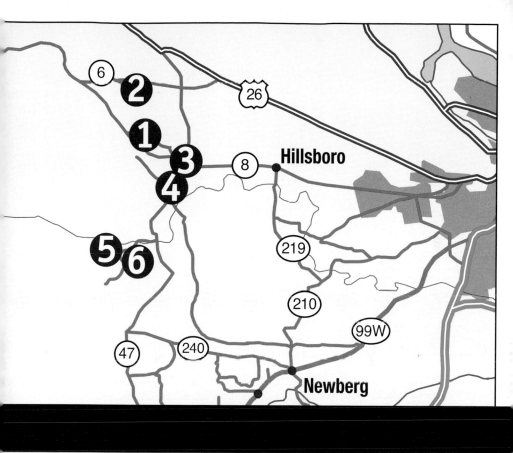

David Hill Vineyard & Winery

46350 David Hill Road
P.O. Box 366
Forest Grove, OR 97116
503-992-8545
877-992-8545

davidhill.winery@verizon.net

Hours

12p.m.-5p.m. Tues.-Sun.

Winemaker: Pascal Valadier

Owners: Milan and Jean Stoyanov

Vineyard plantings: Pinot noir, Riesling, Pinot gris, Chardonnay, Gewürztraminer

... Directions: From Portland follow Sunset Hwy. (US 26) westbound to the North Plains exit (#57). Exit to the right then turn left and cross the freeway. Proceed south on Glencoe Rd., about 1 mile. At the light turn right on Zion Church Rd. and continue about 3 more miles until you come to a stop sign. Turn right on Verboort Road. This road turns into Purdin Rd. Go straight to Thatcher Rd. and turn left. Go to David Hill Road, turn right, and continue on the gravel road. The winery is on your left.

The Stoyanovs have owned the David Hill property since November 1992. The winery is known by the locals for its Farm House White, a combination of Chardonnay, Riesling, Pinot blanc, and Gewürztraminer.

Driving up the steep hill to the winery, your first glance is a beautiful restored 1883 farm house. This turn-of-the-century house is painted a fresh pansy yellow with crisp white

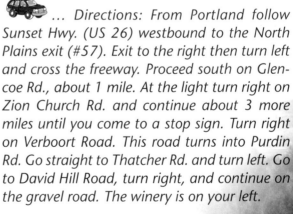

windowsills. The tasting room has the ambiance of a boutique. Entering the winery, the white square-shaped tasting bar is on your left. Through an archway on your right is the tastefully done gift shop. You will not see the usual tee shirts and wine accessories, but rather fine art, and hand-painted pictures of grapes on antique linens such as table-cloths and aprons. It is like being in a muse-um! Every detail of the house has been attended to, even down to the doorknobs and towel racks in the bathroom. A beautiful restoration job! The house sits on the top of David Hill and overlooks 40 acres of vine-yards. There is plenty of room to roam around and lounge outside if you wish.

Debra's Choices:

Farm House White and Red

Pinot Noir Reserve

Tualatin Estate

10850 NW Seavey Rd.
Forest Grove, OR 97116
503-357-5005

Hours:

Noon-5 p.m. Saturday and Sunday or by appointment. Closed January and February.

barbara@sao.org

Winemaker Joe Dobbes

Vineyard plantings: Pinot noir, Pinot blanc, Chardonnay, Riesling, and Gewürztraminer

This trek will take about 20 minutes from David Hill. It is well worth the effort, as you wind around tree-laden hills and up and down gravel roads that overlook the valley.

... Directions: From David Hill Winery—From the driveway turn right on David Hill Rd. Go down the mountain, turn left on Thatcher Rd., then turn left on Clapshaw Hill Rd. You will continue for two miles on a gravel road. The winery is on the right.

Tualatin is a tasting room only, with all the wine production at their parent company, the Willamette Valley Winery. The tasting room is very spacious, and there is ample seating room outside.

This winery is not your typical Oregon estate winery. It is low-key and unassuming–until you taste the Pinot noir. Then you are in for a real treat. Tualatin Estate Vineyards has been around since 1973 and is one of the oldest estates in Oregon, with 140 acres of wine grapes. The winemaker, Joe

Dobbes, is known internationally. His 1998 Pinot noir is rich, juicy, and very velvety, with round tannins. You must buy a bottle if they have any left. 1998 was a good year for Pinot noirs because the crop levels were down 30-50% due to a cold, rainy spring. (The grapes harvested contain more soil nutrients.) If you can't make it to this winery you can taste the Pinots at the Willamette Valley Vineyards.

Debra's Choice:
Tualatin Estate Pinot Noir—any vintage will be great

Momokawa Saké/SakéOne

820 Elm Street
Forest Grove, OR 97116
503-357-7056

info@momokawa.com

www.sakeone.com

Hours:
Tasting room open noon to 5 p.m. daily.
Saké Kura tours noon to 2 p.m. Saturdays.

MOMOKAWA
PREMIUM SAKÉ

Moonstone

The world's
first infused
sakés

Saké One
MASTERS OF SAKE

WELCOME 歓 迎

🚙 *... From Tualatin turn left out of the driveway onto Clapshaw Hill Rd. Turn right on Kansas City Rd. Turn left on Purdin Rd., cross over Hwy 47, and turn right on Martin Rd. Go until you reach Hwy 47 again (it loops around the town) and turn left on the hwy. Continue straight following signs to McMinnville. Watch for Elm St. and turn left. You will see SakéOne.*

Don't ask! I know it is not grape wine, but this is one of the best saké houses in the U.S.

The saké brewery is three years old and it is the only American-owned saké kura out of 1,800 worldwide. The brewery has four traditional chilled premium sakés and four infused chilled premium sakés. We tried the Pearl with coconut aroma. It was different and very good.

Montinore Estate

3663 SW Dilley Road
P.O. Box 490
Forest Grove, OR 97116
503-359-5012

Hours:

11a.m.-5p.m. daily for tasting, early June-Dec; weekends only, Jan.-May. Store open year-round. Tours weekends. Closed on major holidays

www.montinore.com

Winemaker: Jacques Tardy

Owners: Montinore Vineyards Ltd.

Vineyard plantings: Pinot noir Pinot gris, Chardonnay, Riesling, Gewürztraminer and Müller-Thurgau

 ... Directions: From SakéOne go back to Hwy 47 and turn left. In about a half mile you will see signs for Montinore. Turn right on Dudney St., turn right on Dilley Rd. and continue past the school. Turn left into Montinore Estate.

Well, this is the real deal. Montinore is a 585-acre estate owned by Leo and Jane Graham. The original Dilley Mansion was built in 1905. (The Dilleys built the entire town at the turn of the century.) Across from the mansion is the unique lodge-like winery surrounded by a beautifully manicured garden. The spacious tasting room has a gorgeous view of the Cascade Range mountains and it is definitely a retreat—a place where you forget about your weight, your mortgage, or a child who is flunking out of school.

This is one of the larger wineries in Oregon with a yearly production of up to 40,000 cases. After wine tasting, stroll the grounds for awhile and take in the gardens before you go on to your next winery.

Debra's Choices:
Graham's Block 7 Single Vineyard Pinot Noir

Riesling

Elk Cove Vineyards

27751 NW Olson Rd.
Gaston, OR 97119
503-985-7760

elkcove@teleport.com

www.elkcove.com

Hours:
11a.m. to 5 p.m. daily. Closed Christmas Eve and Day, Thanksgiving Day and New Year's Day.

Owners: Joe and Patricia Campbell

Winemakers: Adam Campbell/James Cahill

Vineyard plantings: Pinot noir, Pinot gris, Riesling, Pinot blanc, Gewürztraminer, Viognier

... Directions: From Montinore, go back to Hwy 47 and turn right. Go past the town of Gaston. Turn right on Olsen Rd. and go to the top of the hill, about 3 miles.

The winery was founded in 1973 by Joe and Pat who picked out this land that is thick with wildflowers and plum trees. The grounds surrounding the winery are well maintained, yet have a sense of unruliness, letting nature make its own beauty. The winery sits on the hilltop, but assumes its position without overpowering the hill or its neighbors. The amphitheater-like building with panoramic views from the large picture window blends into the scenery, becoming one with the environment. There is nothing pretentious about this winery, yet it is elegant. I felt like I was surrounded by a Frank Lloyd Wright inspiration.

Elk Cove is particularly devoted to designating their vineyards to specific varietals. Pinot noir is what this winery is noted for and they have three vineyards dedicated to this grape. We tried several of their single vineyard wines, and one in particular that I just loved is the 1998 Pinot noir, Windhill Vineyard. Cheryl enjoyed the German-style Estate Riesling, with strong floral aromas. The *Wine Spectator* gave 90 points for the 1998 Pinot noir, La Boheme Vineyard. Don't leave this winery without buying your favorite choice of wine, because you may not have the opportunity again!

Debra's Choices:
Pinot Noir Windhill

Pinot Gris, Willamette Valley

Estate Riesling

Kramer Vineyards

26830 NW Olson Rd.
Gaston, OR 97119
503-662-4545

info@kramerwine.com

www.kramerwine.com

Hours:

Open noon to 5 p.m. daily, June through Sept.; noon to 5 p.m. Fri.-Sun., March through Dec. Closed January and February, Easter and Christmas.

Owners: Trudy and Keith Kramer

Winemaker: Trudy Kramer

Vineyard plantings: Pinot noir, Pinot gris, Müller-Thurgau, Chardonnay, Carmina

The tasting room is small, so I recommend that you sample your wine, buy a glass and take it out on the veranda which overlooks the valley. Take in the grazing sheep, beautiful farmland, and tranquility of an Alpine afternoon. This winery is enjoyable and Trudy is funny and personable. She offers a unique collection of painted wine glasses for sale.

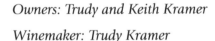

Debra's Choice:
Müller-Thurgau

Wine tasting notes…

Wine
and vintage: _____

Tasted when and where: _____

Price: $ _____

Tasting notes: _____

Wine and vintage: _____

Tasted when and where: _____

Price: $ _____

Tasting notes: _____

Wine and vintage: _____

Tasted when and where: _____

Price: $ _____

Tasting notes: _____

Wine and vintage: _____

Tasted when and where: _____

Price: $ _____

Tasting notes: _____

TOUR 2

After Tour 1 Cheryl and I went to McMinn-ville. It was only 5p.m.—too early to think about dinner. So we stopped at a wine bar called Noah's. No, we were not tired of wines by that point. Actually, we wanted to relax and have a glass, because we had been spitting out wine all day. It was just by luck that we stopped in at this wonderful bar. The owner, Jack Thornton, is very knowledgeable about Oregon wines. Additionally, Neil Thompson, a wine distributor and self-proclaimed "winegeek," was sitting at the bar taking orders. We talked for two hours about Oregon wines and sampled many. Jack made us warm brie on bread to go with our wines and conversation. We begrudgingly walked away from this enlightening conversation and went next door to Nick's Italian Café (recommended by all the locals), and we were soon eating one of the best meals that I have ever had.

This tour runs down Hwy 99 and the wineries are either across or down the street from one another. This makes it convenient because you can't get lost. I loved this tour and was enchanted by the small towns that meander around Hwy 99. The wineries on this tour each have their own special style. They are charming, unique, and most importantly, welcoming. Most of these wineries have their vineyards on the Red Hills of Dundee where some of the best Pinot noir in North America is grown.

Tour 2 takes two to three days.

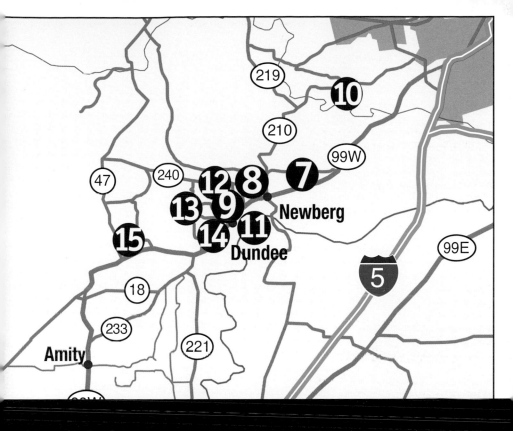

Rex Hill Vineyards

30835 N. Highway 99W
Newberg, OR 97132
503-538-0666
info@rexhill.com

www.rexhill.com

Hours

10 a.m. to 5 p.m. Friday-Sunday, Memorial Day through Thanksgiving. Winter hours are 11 a.m. to 5 p.m. daily. Closed major holidays.

Owners: Paul Hart and Jan Jacobsen

Winemaker: Aron Hess

Vineyard plantings: Pinot noir, Pinot gris, and Chardonnay

... *Directions: From Newberg take 99 West and you will see the winery sign. Turn right, go up the hill and around to the front.*

The winery is unique among wineries in this area. The building is painted gunmetal grey

and has a long narrow rectangular shape. When coming up the hill you are greeted by the back of the stark building. Once you are in inside, it is a completely different experience, with polished wooden floors graced with oriental rugs, and oversized ornate tables with books, posters, and wine accessories beautifully displayed. But most surprising are two long, narrow tunnels that are right off the tasting room. The first tunnel is an Oregon Wine Brotherhood Museum with well-dressed mannequins clothed in period pieces from the Brotherhood. Next to this is a tunnel with wine barrels dark enough to impart the feeling of a 12th century monastery.

There is a well-groomed picnic area on the premises to enjoy the surrounding Chehalem Mountains. The staff is well informed and very friendly, so feel free to ask a lot of questions. To give you an idea of how spectacular Rex Hill's wines are, the *Spectator* gave 90 points for their 1999 Pinot noir.

Debra's Choices:
2000 Willamette Pinot Gris

2000 Kings Ridge Pinot Noir

Duck Pond Cellars

23145 Hwy 99W
P.O. Box 429
Dundee, OR 97115
503-538-3199/800-437-3213

duckpond@duckpondcellars.com

www.duckpondcellars.com

Hours:

10 a.m. to 5 p.m.
May through Oct./
11 a.m. to 5 p.m.
Nov. through April.

Owners: The Fries and Jenkins Families

Winemaker: Greg Fries

Vineyard plantings: Pinot noir and Pinot gris in Oregon; Chardonnay, Merlot, Syrah, and Gewürztraminer in Washington.

... Directions: From Rex Hill turn right on 99 West, go through the town of Newberg and the winery is on the right, just off 99. Watch carefully for the signs.

The winery is spacious, and is surrounded by flowering plum trees. It has a seating area in the front with a pond—and you guessed it—ducks!! The terrace is comfortable and is under an oak tree that shields you from the highway's traffic.

Duck Pond Winery has vineyards

and facilities in two states. They produce up to 90,000 cases of wine annually. This can be easily done with their 300 acres in Oregon and 540 acres in Washington.

Debra's Choices:

2000 Chardonnay, Columbia Valley; it is creamy and not too much oak.

2000 Merlot Columbia Valley

Dundee Springs Winery, Perry Bower Vineyard

9605 Fox Farm Rd.
P.O. Box 9
Dundee, OR 97115
503-554-8000

sales@dundeesprings.com

www.dundeesprings.com

Hours:
Open 11-5 daily except Easter, Fourth of July and the week between Christmas and New Year's.

Owner: Mary Lynne Perry

Winemaker: Jim Kakacek

Vineyard plantings: Pinot noir, Pinot gris, and Pinot blanc

 ... Directions: from Duck Pond to

Dundee get back on 99 West heading south and turn right on Sunny Crest just off of 99.

Upon entering the driveway, I thought that I was approaching a dreamy 1930s vintage beach house. The house is too charming! Even their labels are cute, but there is nothing too sweet about their Pinots. They are seriously delicious. The Perrys market the winery as "The House of Three Pinots." They produce a mere 3000 cases each year, however they sell most of their fruit from the 60-acre Perry Bower Vineyard to other winemakers. Their best selling variety is Pinot noir.

Dundee Springs has a "demonstration vineyard" right out the back door. You can pick the grapes yourself, or just meander through the vineyard and pretend to be a vintner.

Debra's Choices:

1999 Pinot Gris; a crisp, appley, balanced wine.

2000 Pinot Blanc; start your meal with this wine.

Ponzi Vineyards

14665 Southwest Winery Lane
Beaverton, OR 97007
503-628-1227

info@ponziwines.com

www.ponziwines.com

Hours:
Open daily from 11 a.m. to 5 p.m. during the week and from noon to 5 p.m. on the weekends.

Owners: Dick and Nancy Ponzi

Vineyard plantings: Pinot noir, Pinot gris, Chardonnay, Pinot blanc, Dolcetto, and Riesling

... *Directions: Back on 99 West head south, and Ponzi is about 1/2 mile down on your right.*

Ponzi winery is FUN and more FUN, with a large tasting room, a classy wine bar and

unlike many area wineries, they even provide stools to sit on. What I especially appreciated were the Riedel glasses for wine tasting. The wine bar has many other Oregon wines in their tasting room for sale as well. So if you missed an opportunity to buy at a winery, don't despair—you can probably buy it at Ponzi's. The bar's menu includes lunch and snack items, and some great cheeses. Separate from the wine bar is the estate vineyard which also has a tasting room.

There is an adjacent restaurant that offers wonderful meals. Cheryl and I ate there twice, it was so good.

The Ponzis have helped shape the Oregon wine industry and lobbied for some of the toughest labeling requirements in the country. Nancy Ponzi co-founded the International Pinot Noir Celebration, the Salud Pinot Noir Auction and Oregon Pinot Camp. The Ponzis have played an important role in helping put Oregon's wine on the map of success.

Debra's Choices:

2000 Pinot Gris

1999 Pinot Noir Reserve
(Spectator gave this wine 93 points.)

Argyle Winery

691 Highway 99W
P.O. Box 280
Dundee, OR 97115
503-538-8520/888-4ARGYLE

buywine@argylewinery.com

www.argylewinery.com

Hours:
11 a.m. to 5 p.m. every day
but major holidays.

Owner: Lion Nathan

Winemaker: Rollin Soles

*Vineyard plantings: Pinot noir, Chardonnay, and
Riesling*

... Directions: Located on Hwy 99 West
in Dundee, just across the street from Ponzi.

The tasting room is small and housed in what
used to be the parlor of a Victorian home.
Argyle is surprisingly unpretentious consider-
ing Rollin Soles
is a premier
winemaker in
the U.S. and
you are in *his*
winery, tasting
outstanding
wines.

This is a serious
winery and they
can claim many
reviews from
Spectator for
their sparkling
and still wines.

Argyle can boast of 400 acres of vineyards and they produce 35,000 cases annually. You can see some production outside when you visit. The winery is known in Oregon for their sparkling wines such as Brut and Blanc de Blanc. However, they also produce some knock-out Pinot noir. They charge a dollar for tasting, but this is a small price to pay for quality wine.

Debra's Choice:

Any sparkling wines

1999 Reserve Willamette Valley

Lange Winery

18380 NE Buena Vista
P.O. Box 8
Dundee, OR 97115
503-538-6476

www.langewinery.com

Hours:

11 a.m. to 5 p.m. daily; closed on Tuesdays.

Owners: Don and Wendy Lange

Winemakers: Don Lange and Jesse Lange

Vineyard plantings: Pinot noir, Pinot gris, Pinot blanc, Chardonnay

... Directions: *Again head south on Hwy 99 West to West 9th Street and head up the hill. Turn right on Warden Hills and head up the hill again. Follow the blue winery signs.*

Lange Winery has the most spectacular view of all the wineries. Sit outside on the veranda, sip a superb Pinot noir, and take in the views of Mt. Hood and Mt. Jefferson. The sun could be beating down on your head, but just eyeing these majestic, snow-covered peaks cools your heels.

The Langes are fond of saying "dry wine, dry humor," and that is exactly right. They are a wonderful and funny family. The winery was founded in 1987 by the Langes who now produce over 7,000 cases annually from their 30-acre estate in the Red Hills of Dundee.

Don is not your usual winemaker/proprietor. He is a poet; a graduate from the University of Iowa Writer's Workshop, which is very difficult to get into. He has turned his poetry into songs, now compiled on several CDs. They are for sale in the winery and in music stores. He also finds time to fly fish—hence the labels.

It is his wines that you must go to Lange's Winery for, particularly the Pinot noir, from any of his designated vineyards.

Debra's Choices:

2000 Pinot Gris Yamhill Vineyards

1999 Pinot Noir Three Hill Cuvee, (this is represented at the International Pinot Noir Celebration)

Erath Vineyards

9409 NE Worden Hill Road
Dundee, OR 97115
503-538-3318/800-539-9463

info@erath.com

www.erath.com

Hours:

10:30 a.m. to 5:30 p.m. daily, May 15
through Oct. 15; 11 a.m. to 5 p.m. daily
Oct. 16 through May 14

Owner: Dick Erath

Winemaker: Rob Stuart

*Vineyard plantings: Pinot noir, Pinot gris,
Chardonnay, Pinot blanc, Dolcetto*

... Directions: From Lange to Erath get
back to Warden Hills Rd. and turn right. Head
down and around the hill, and Erath is on the
left.

Getting to Erath is a beautiful journey
through the Red Hills of Dundee. Dick Erath
is one of the early pioneers in Willamette Valley who put stakes down to prove that Pinot
noir could grow in Oregon. In 1969 he plant-

ed his first vines in the Chehalem Hills. Just four years later his Pinot noirs were winning gold medals. Today the winery produces 35,000 cases of wine annually, of which two thirds is Pinot noir. Sample some of the single vineyard wines. If you want an inexpensive table wine buy the Oregon Pinot Noir, and have it with Oregon salmon.

Tourists have fun here. The atmosphere is light and all about sampling good wine.

Debra's Choices:

1998 Pinot Noir Reserve Willamette Valley

2000 Pinot Gris

Sokol Blosser Winery

P.O. Box 399
5000 Sokol Blosser Lane
Dundee, OR 97115
503-864-2282

info@sokolblosser.com

www.sokolblosser.com

Hours:

11 a.m. to 5 p.m. daily.

*Owners: Susan Sokol Blosser
and Bill Blosser*

Winemaker: Russ Rosner

Vineyard plantings: Pinot noir, Pinot gris, Müller-Thurgau, Riesling, and Chardonnay

... Directions: From Erath to Sokol Blosser go back down the hill to 99 West, turn right and then another right on Sokol Blosser Lane. You can't miss it!

This winery has stayed true to the environment. It is surrounded by Oregon wildflowers and trees. The tasting room is a good size and they have ample seating outside on a front deck with views of Mt. Hood and Willamette Valley. The employees are polite and knowledgeable. Sokol Blosser is family owned and operated. They have an unusual visitor's self-guided tour through the vineyards that explains the wine grape varieties and describes the different seasons of the vineyard. If you want to learn more about what you are drinking, then this is the place to take the tour.

Debra's Choices:
1998 Pinot Noir Willamette Valley

2000 Pinot Gris Willamette Valley

Chateau Benoit

Chateau Benoit

9580 NE Mineral Springs Rd.
Carlton, OR 97111
503-864-2991

www.chateaubenoit.com

Hours:
Open daily all year, excluding major holidays.

Owner: Columbia Empire Farms

Winemaker: Scott Huffman

Vineyard plantings: Riesling, Müller-Thurgau, Pinot noir, Pinot gris, Chardonnay

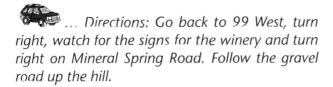 ... Directions: Go back to 99 West, turn right, watch for the signs for the winery and turn right on Mineral Spring Road. Follow the gravel road up the hill.

Wow! This outstanding view is to die for. Sitting majestically on the hilltop beckoning wine tasters, the winery overlooks the entire Willamette Valley, and there are plenty of benches scattered among the gardens for you to sit, relax, and sip the wine. However, don't get too philosophical about nature's beauty. You also need to go inside and breathe in the elegance. Please do not miss this winery on your tour—you will regret it!

The winery is switching its focus from white to red wines, all selected from the Pinot noir clones, and they are reducing the crop output of these particular vines to make a more intense fruit. Look for the vineyard-designated wines such as Yamhill, Doe Ridge, and Kestrel.

Debra's Choice:
2000 Pinot noir Willamette Valley

Wine tasting notes…

Wine and vintage: _____

Tasted when and where: _____

Price: $ _____

Tasting notes: _____

✺🍇

Wine and vintage: _____

Tasted when and where: _____

Price: $ _____

Tasting notes: _____

✺🍇

Wine and vintage: _____

Tasted when and where: _____

Price: $ _____

Tasting notes: _____

✺🍇

Wine and vintage: _____

Tasted when and where: _____

Price: $ _____

Tasting notes: _____

✺🍇

TOUR 3

We started out from Salem on this tour because we wanted to make sure that Willamette Valley Winery wasn't missed. This tour is around the Eola Hills and is surrounded by Mt. Hood and Mt. Jefferson. Most, if not all the wineries are on hilltops overlooking the Willamette Valley. Even if you only wanted to spend a couple hours wine tasting, any of these wineries would provide the ambiance and good wine to finish the day.

Tour takes around six hours.

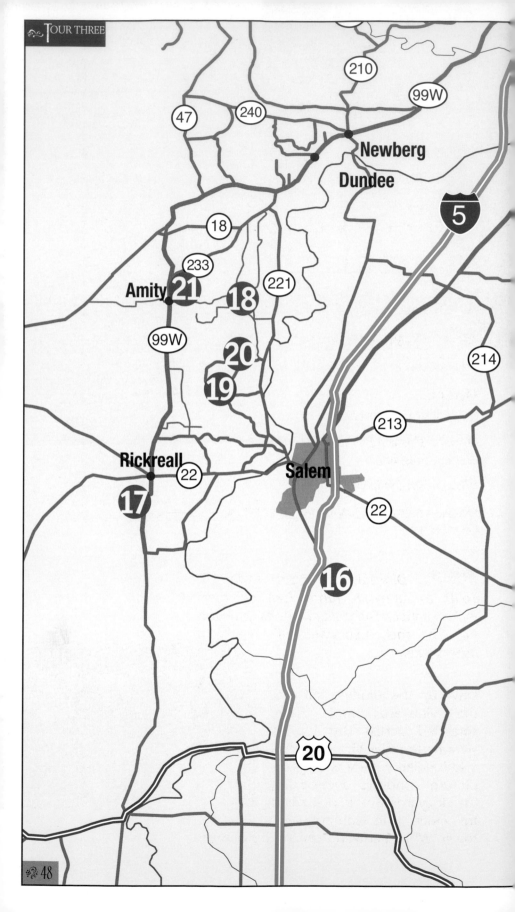

Willamette Valley Vineyards

8800 Enchanted Way SE
Turner, OR 97392
503-588-9463/800-344-9463

www.wvv.com

Hours:
Call for appointment

Owners: This is a publicly held winery/Jim Bernau, President

Winemaker: Joe Dobbes

Vineyard plantings: Pinot noir, Pinot gris, and Chardonnay

... Directions: from Salem take I-5 South to Sunnyside Turne. Turn left, then make a right on Enchanted Way and go up the hill. The enchanted gates will usher you in.

Drive up the winding hill past the vineyards and there, sprawled across the hill, is Willamette Valley Vineyards. It is a lodge-like winery with giant picture windows overlooking the vineyards. The trademark of the winery is its looming water tower. When I arrived I saw visions of King

Arthur riding up the hill to greet me. Oh well, a girl can dream, right? The winery is spacious and welcoming. The facility is set up for hosting many functions, including weddings, banquets or any special occasion that you can think of.

Of the estate's 75 acres, 55 are dedicated to three varietals: Pinot noir, Pinot gris and Chardonnay. Winemaker Dobbes' Signature Cuvee was credited in 2001 by *Wine Enthusiast Magazine* as one of the top 100 wines in the world. Willamette also owns Griffin Creek Vineyards and Tualitan Estate.

Debra's choices:
2000 Pinot Gris Griffin Creek Rogue Valley

2000 Founder's Reserve Willamette Valley Vineyards

Eola Hills
Wine Cellars, Inc.

501 S. Pacific Highway W.
Rickreall, OR 97371
503-623-2405

tom-huggins@eolahillswinery.com

www.eolahillswinery.com

Hours:
11 a.m. to 5 p.m. daily

Founder: Tom Huggins

Winemaker: Steve Anderson

Vineyard plantings: Pinot noir, Chardonnay, Sauvignon blanc, Pinot gris, Viognier, Marechal Foch

🚙 *... Directions: From Salem take 22 West to a stoplight, about 10 miles. Turn left on 99 West going toward Rickreall. The winery is on your right.*

A family-owned operation, Eola Hills Wine Cellars is a place that you want to go and buy cases of wine. They produce very good quality table wines at a reasonable price. The wine bar is almost part of the production room. While we were sampling the wine, we watched the bottling process—and it wasn't through glass windows!

On Sundays in August they have bicycle tours incorporating nearby wineries. The 45-mile loop starts and ends at Eola Hills. This ride costs $50.00 per person which includes lunch and dinner at the wineries.

They produce 10,000 cases annually and they own 117 acres of vineyards. Their best vintages are 1999 and 2000. Don't leave without a bottle of Chardonnay.

Debra's Choices:

1999 Pinot Noir

Chardonnay

Bethel Heights Vineyard

6060 Bethel Heights Rd. NW
Salem, OR 97304
503-581-2262

info@bethelheights.com

www.bethelheights.com

Hours:

11 a.m. to 5 p.m Sat. and Sun., March-May;. Tues. through Sun., June-Sept.; Sat. and Sun.; Oct.-Nov. Closed Dec. through Feb. except by appointment. Closed holidays.

Owners: Terry Casteel, Marilyn Webb, Ted Casteel, Pat Dudley and Barbara Dudley

Winemaker: Terry Casteel

Vineyard plantings: Pinot noir, Chardonnay, Pinot gris, Pinot blanc

 *... Go back out to 99 West, turn right on Bethel Rd. (First flashing yellow light north of Hwy. 18), and you will see signs to Bethel Heights Winery.*

This winery is one of the best on the tour for visitors. It has that Oregon lodge look with a steep roof, wooden frame, enormous windows and a vast deck. Its immense tasting room offers a panoramic view. You will be missing a rare treat if you don't stop here, buy a glass and take it to their deck. In the front, there are sheep grazing on very green grass, and in the back are vineyards going down the slopes to the valley. You can't tire of the view. If you need to do some soulful contemplating, stop here, and by the second glass, your problems will all be solved.

They have 49 acres of vineyards right outside the door. And of course the best selling varietal is the Pinot noir. Their best vintages are 1991, 1993, 1999 and they just released their 2000.

Debra's Choices:

1999 Estate Pinot Noir

Pinot Noir Southeast Block Reserve

Cristom

6905 Spring Valley Rd. NW
Salem, OR 97304
503-375-3068

winery@cristomwines.com

Winemaker: Steve Doerner

Owners: Paul and Eileen Gerrie

Vineyard plantings: Viognier, Pinot noir, Pinot gris and Chardonnay

... *Directions: From Bethel Heights go to the bottom of the road, turn left, and go about four miles until the next intersection. Turn left on Spring Valley Rd., go up the hill and watch for winery signs on your left.*

Cristom is all about making good wine. They have a beautiful facility and if you sit outside, you can take in the

view of Mt. Hood and Mt. Jefferson. A real treat.

Current annual production is 7,500 cases. They incorporate the Old World style—with French oak barrels throughout their cellar. Their vineyards are designated for one varietal, which is becoming increasingly common in Oregon to reflect the vineyard terroir (that mysterious combination of soil qualities, climate, terrain, and loving care that impart subtle nuances to the wine.)

In March 2002, Cristom was named an Oregon Fruit-of-the-Vine Power by *Decanter Magazine*, published in London. Winemaker Doerner's Pinot noir receives a lot of recognition from *Wine Spectator* as well. If you can't get to the winery you can order online, however, it is worth the extra effort to make it there. Try the 1998 Reserve Willamette Valley. Wow! Is it good—with black fruits, a spicy nose and long aftertaste.

Debra's Choices:

1998 Mt. Jefferson Cuvee Willamette Valley

1999 Pinot Noir Reserve Willamette Valley

Witness Tree Vineyard

7111 Spring Valley Rd NW
Salem, OR 97304
503-585-7874/888-478-8766

info@witnesstreevineyard.com

www.witnesstreevineyard.com

Hours:

11 a.m. to 5 p.m. Sat.-Sun., March through May; Tues.-Sun., June through Aug.; Sat.-Sun., Sept. through Dec.

Owners: Dennis and Carolyn Devine

Winemaker: Bryce Bagnall

Directions: This winery is next door to Cristom on Spring Valley Road. Turn left out of Cristom's driveway, and go about 1/2 mile north on Spring Valley Rd.

Vineyard plantings: Pinot noir, Chardonnay, Viognier, Pinot blanc, Lagrein, Dolcetto

The winery is marked by the ancient oak Witness Tree, an Oregon landmark. The Devines let this tree be the center of attention. This is a small but quaint winery. It is like

visiting a petite farm house. In the summer, beautiful pots of flowers offset the rugged terrain.

Debra's Choice:
1999 Pinot Noir
Willamette Valley

Amity Vineyards

18150 Amity Vineyards Rd.
Amity, OR 97101
503-835-2362

amity@amityvineyards.com

www.amityvineyards.com

Hours:

12 p.m. to 5 p.m. daily; closed Christmas Day and all of January.

Owners; Myron Redford and Victoria Wettle

Winemaker: Myron Redford

Vineyard plantings: Gamay noir, Pinot noir, Pinot blanc, Riesling

... *Directions: From Witness Tree, go right onto Spring Valley Rd. At the first stop sign make a right onto Zena Rd., go seven miles, make a right on 99 West and watch for signs for Amity. You'll turn right, then left onto the first dirt road. It is well marked.*

I walked into the tasting room, a corner of the building painted Tuscany-style red. The wine tasting manager, Dianna Hrabik started serving me excellent Pinot noir and chocolates to melt away my stress. It worked, and before long we were taking a walk together. She looked at me with her steel blue eyes and said "Anytime I turn an uptight person into a smiling person, I'm happy." (Who, *me*?)

She has a quote: "We're not real fancy but we're close to funky." They are funky, but those of us who went through the 70s together will feel right at home.

This is a fun place to end your tour! And if you are uptight, she will loosen you up!

Debra's Choices:

2000 Gamay Noir; *"drink this with a plate of sp'getti and watch* Wheel of Fortune.*"*
Dianna Hrabik

2000 Dry Riesling; *"least offensive for the most amount of wine"* Dianna Hrabik

Wine tasting notes...

Wine and vintage: _____

Tasted when and where: _____

Price: $ _____

Tasting notes: _____

Wine and vintage: _____

Tasted when and where: _____

Price: $ _____

Tasting notes: _____

Wine and vintage: _____

Tasted when and where: _____

Price: $ _____

Tasting notes: _____

Wine and vintage: _____

Tasted when and where: _____

Price: $ _____

Tasting notes: _____

TOUR 4

Tour 4 is at the very end of Willamette Valley and the tour is all about wineries of Lane County. There are eight wineries in Lane County and we chose four to write about. Three of the four are off Territorial Highway and are easy to work into a tour. All of these wineries are dedicated to making good wine and promoting tourism. Each has a different ambiance and different scenery, but all offer excellent wines.

Tour takes about four hours.

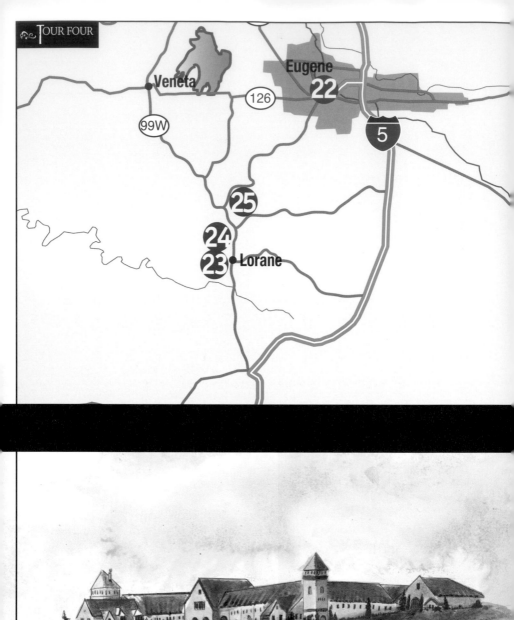

Eugene
22

Veneta

126

99W

25

24
23 • Lorane

5

Eugene Wine Cellars

255 Madison Street
Eugene, OR 97402

ewcmon@aol.com

www.areawine.com

Hours:
Friday 1p.m. to 8 p.m.
Sat. - Sun. 12 p.m. to 6 p.m..

Owner: Bruce Bettina

Vineyard plantings: grapes are purchased from sites around the state, including properties they farm: Pinot noir, Pinot gris, Pinot blanc, Syrah, Viognier, Melon, Chardonnay

... \ *Directions: On Madison in downtown Eugene.*

Sample different wines and then begin your tour, or you can end your tour here and enjoy an entire glass of wine.

Chateau Lorane

27415 Siuslaw River Rd.
Lorane, OR 97451
541-942-8028

linde@chateaulorane.com

www.chateaulorane.com

Hours:
Jan. through May and Oct. through Dec.

– weekends noon to 5 p.m. or by appointment; June through Sept.—daily noon to 5 p.m. or by appointment.

Owners: Linde & Sharon Kester

Winemaker: David Hook

Vineyard plantings: Pinot noir, Marechal Foch, Leon Millot, Pinot Meunier, Riesling, Sauvignon, Various German Hybrids

... Directions: From Eugene, take West 11th Ave. to Bailey Hill Rd/Lorane Hwy. Turn left on Territorial Hwy. and continue on the road for about 10 miles. There will be a country store on your left. Keep going and look for a winery sign on your right. Turn up the road which eventually turns into a gravel road; just keep going and the winery is on a hill.

Lorane Winery's deck overlooks the private 24-acre Lake Louise, which is surrounded by fir-covered hills. There are tables and chairs for wine sippers to relax and hear the running water cascading over the boulders. The winery opened in 1994, and winemaker David Hook crafts unusual wines that are rarely seen on wine menus. Try the Melon de Bourgogne, or Flora and Pinot Meunier. The tasting room has a unique collection of hand-crafted ceramics. Of course, I had to buy a white wine cooler which now sits on my kitchen counter, ready for my next wine and food tasting event.

Debra's Choices:

1998 Marechal Foch

1998 Pinot Meunier

King Estate

80854 Territorial Rd.
Eugene, OR 97405
541-942-9874/800-884-4441

www.kingestate.com

Hours:

12 p.m. to 5 p.m. daily, summer/weekends,
winter

Owners: The King Family

Winemakers: Bill Kremer and Ray Walsh

*Vineyard plantings: Pinot noir, Chardonnay,
Pinot gris*

... *Directions: From Lorane, turn left on
Territorial Highway. Go straight for about three
miles and the winery sits on a hilltop on the
right—you can't miss it.*

This is a real estate, with majestic gates and all. Just the drive through all of the grapevines up a very long hill gets a wine taster ready with high expectations of great wine. You won't be disappointed. The tasting room is small and a new tasting room is being constructed for growing tourism. The grounds are simply breathtaking. I wanted to sit outside in the sun all afternoon sipping their 1998 Pinot Noir Oregon Reserve, a supple Pinot with black cherry aromas and flavors. Buy a bottle for $35.00 and share it with someone who really enjoys wine. In 2001, *Wine Spectator* gave three of their Pinot noirs above 90 pts.

King Estate is one of the better marketers in Oregon. It has gone past pleasing only the locals to national and international distribution, as well. King Estate is doing what California wineries have been doing for the last 20 years—getting their wines past the border. The wines are not overpriced, due to larger volume and wider selling areas. King Estate has only been in business since 1992. Well, move over California.

They have over 800 acres of vineyards, right outside their door, and produce a whopping 80,000 cases annually. Their winemaking facility is quite impressive. Needless to say, we enjoyed ourselves thoroughly and hated to leave such a glorious and pampering winery.

Debra's Choices:

1998 Reserve Oregon Pinot Noir

1998 Oregon Pinot Gris Vin Glace

Hinman Vineyards/ Silvan Ridge

27012 Briggs Hill Rd.
Eugene, OR 97405
541-345-1945

info@silvanridge.com

www.silvanridge.com

Hours:
12 p.m. to 5 p.m. daily, excluding holidays.

Owner: Carolyn Chambers

Winemaker: Bryan Wilson

Vineyard plantings: Pinot gris / They purchase Pinot noir, Riesling, Cabernet Sauvignon, Cabernet Franc, Merlot, Muscat, Syrah, Gewürztraminer, Grenache Rose, Viognier

... Directions: From King Estate, turn left out of the driveway (back toward Hwy 126), go up Territorial Rd. and watch for the winery signs.

After visiting King Estate it is time to catch a glimpse of reality. Hinman was established in 1979 and was the 14th winery in southern Willamette Valley. Carolyn Chambers bought the winery in 1991 from Doyle Hinman and created the Silvan Ridge label for a premium brand. She had the winery remodeled in 1999 depicting a country French interior with tiles and heavy dark wood. It is wonderful. They have a front terrace for sipping and drinking—bring some cheese and crackers with you and stay awhile. This is the place where you feel comfortable bringing your picnic.

TOURS BY APPOINTMENT

Wineries by appointment only

These wineries are worth noting but are not in a tour — they are by appointment only.

If you call all three wineries ahead of time you can make a tour of it because they are in the same general area. Please follow their directions from your location. All of these wineries do very well on a national level.

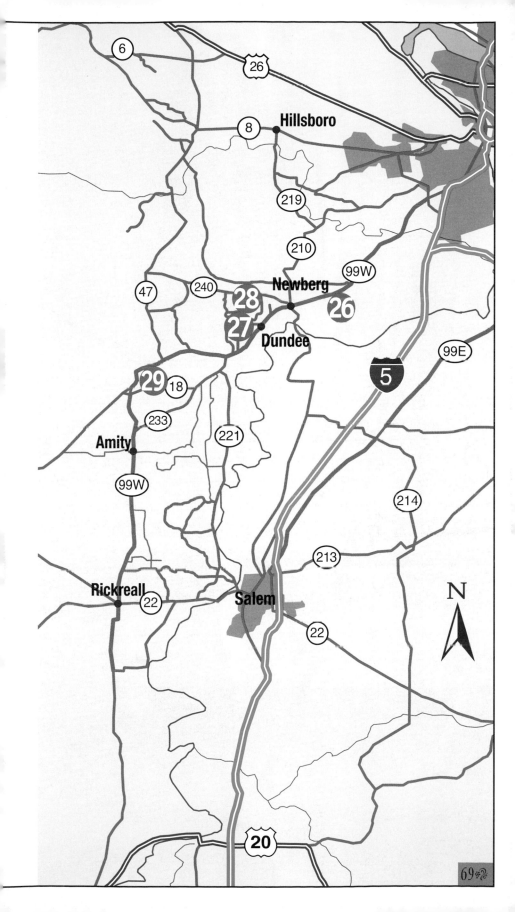

Chehalem

31190 Veritas Lane
Newberg, OR 97132
503-538-4700

Kellyk@chehalemwines.com

www.chehalemwines.com

Winemaker: Harry Peterson-Nedry and Cheryl Francis

Chehalem likes people to visit their winery, and they are by appointment only because they want that one-on-one connection. Chehalem's wine is wonderful, and Kelly Karr, the tasting manager, is knowledgeable about the industry and Chehalem wines—and she loves her work.

We tried and absolutely loved the Pinot Noir, Rion Reserve, the 2000 Pinot Gris Reserve, and the 2000 3-Vineyard Pinot Noir.

Cameron Winery

8200 Worden Hill Rd
Dundee OR 97115
503-538-0336

Winemaker: John Paul

Cameron is marketing its winery on technique: using "non-irrigation" in the vineyards like French viticulturists—to have more authentic wines that best represent the soil's qualities. Cameron has an underground cellar that is similar to a dungeon; dark and musty, like the French cellars of the 15th century.

Everything is worth trying here, but we had 2000 Pinot Noir Clos Electrique. Outstanding, and if I wrote for a wine enthusiast's magazine, I would give this wine 95 points. We drank this right from the barrels.

John Paul developed a Northern Italian-style white wine with Pinot bianco grapes which he calls "Giovanni." He adds an "i" to Cameron (hence Cameroni) to pay homage to the elusive Italian side of the Cameron clan. This wine has developed somewhat of a cult following in Seattle. He is also starting to work with the famous red grape, Nebbiolo, of Barolo.

Domaine Drouhin

PO Box 700
Dundee Oregon 97115
503-864-2700

info@domainedrouhin.com

Winemaker: Veronique Drouhin

In the late 1980s, Maison Joseph Drouhin of Burgundy, France, built a winery in Oregon's Pinot noir country. The winemaker, Veronique Drouhin-Boss, is the fourth generation of Drouhin winemakers. The Drouhins were the first in Oregon to plant their almost-90 acres of vineyard on rootstock to protect the vines from phylloxera, a pest which is

becoming an increasing problem in Oregon and California. Their coopers in Burgundy custom-craft their barrels. Veronique commutes between Beaune, France, and Dundee. Domaine Drouhin opened its doors to visitors in 2001. Tony, the hospitality manager, is informed and friendly.

We love and reccommend the 1998 Laurene/Oregon. Rich and intense — a great meal wine. The 2000 Chardonnay is crisp and very aromatic.

Westrey Wine Company

1065 NE Alpine St.
McMinnville, Oregon 97128
503-434-6357

info@Westrey.com

Winemakers: David Autrey and Amy Wesselman

*Production 3000 cases. Est.1993
First wines released 1994*

In 2000, this husband and wife team purchased an abandoned 50-acre vineyard in the Dundee Hills. They are co-winemakers with a combined experience of 20 years. Their wines are sold nationally.

Wesselman is currently the managing director of the annual International Pinot Noir Celebration.

Debra's Choices
2000 Pinot Noir Willamette Valley

1999 Pinot Noir Reserve

North Willamette Valley—Portland Area

Information

Forest Grove Chamber of Commerce
2417 Pacific Avenue
Forest Grove, OR 97116
Phone: 503-357-3006
Web site: www.fgchamber.com

Sherwood Chamber of Commerce
P.O. Box 805
Sherwood, OR 97140
Phone: 503-625-4207
Web site: www.sherwoodchamber.org

Portland Chamber of Commerce
221 NW Second
Portland, OR 97209
Phone: 503-228-9411

Places to Stay

The Partridge Farm
4300 E. Portland Road
Newberg, OR 97132
Phone: 503-538-2050
Web site: www.rexhill.com

A lovely bed and breakfast on five gorgeous land-scaped acres, furnished with period antiques.

The Vineyard
8115 N.E. Worden Hill Road
Dundee, OR 97115
Phone: 503-538-8705
French country inn with Jacuzzi bathtubs, charming garden and serene pond.

Wine Country Farm
6855 Breyman Orchards Road
Dayton, OR 97114
Phone: 503-864-3446
Toll Free: 800-261-3446
Web site: www.winecountryfarm.com

This French-style home has a spectacular view of the Willamette Valley.

Mattey House
10221 N.E. Mattey Lane
McMinnville, OR 97128
Phone: 503-434-5058
Web site: www.matteyhouse.com

A Queen Anne mansion perfect for relaxation.

Youngberg Hill Inn
10660 S.W. Youngberg Hill Road
McMinnville, OR 97128
Phone: 503-472-2727
Toll Free: 888-657-8668
Web site: www.youngberghill.com

Each room offers a wonderful view of the land. Perfect for peace or a romantic getaway.

Places to Eat

Joel Palmer House Restaurant
600 Ferry Street Box 594
Dayton, OR 97114
Phone: 503-864-2995
Menu features seafood and great desserts.

Nick's Italian Cuisine
521 N.E. Third Street
McMinnville, OR 97128
Phone: 503-434-4471
Northern Italian cuisine.

Red Hills Provincial Dining
276 Highway 99W.
Dundee, OR 97115
Phone: 503-538-8224
Northwest Best Places gives 3 stars

Yamhill Grill
2818 Portland Road
Newberg, OR 97132
Phone: 503-537-2900
Family dining.

Cornerstone Coffee
216 N.E. Third Street
McMinnville, OR 97128
Phone: 503-472-6622

Fresh Palate Café
On Highway 18 between
McMinnville and Sheridan
Phone: 503-843-4400
Full breakfast and lunch menu includes omelettes, smoked salmon, grilled sandwiches and elegant homemade desserts.

Things to Do

Arbutus Garden Arts
119 W. Main Street
Carlton, OR 97111
Phone: 503-852-6530
Enjoy a gallery, nursery and garden art.

The Book Shop, Inc.
334 N.E. Third Street
McMinnville, OR 97128
Phone: 503-472-7786
Wide selection of books from the Northwest.

Lafayette Schoolhouse Antique Mall
748 Highway 99W.
Lafayette, OR 97127
Phone: 503-864-2720
1920s schoolhouse-turned-antique shop; 100 dealers fill the two-floor building.

Central Willamette Valley—Salem Area

Information

Salem Convention & Visitors Association
1313 Mill Street S.E.
Salem, OR 97301
Phone: 503-581-4325
Toll Free: 800-874-7012
Web site: www.scva.org

Places to Stay

Water Street Inn
421 N. Water Street
Silverton, OR 97381
Phone: 503-873-3344
Toll Free: 866-873-3344
Web site: www.thewaterstreetinn.com
Located in historic downtown and close to shopping and restaurants in the area.

Brier Rose Inn Bed & Breakfast
206 Seventh Ave. SW
Albany, OR 97321
Phone: 541-926-0345
This lovely bed and breakfast is close to antique shops.

A Bed and Breakfast on the Green
2515 SW 45th Street
Corvallis, OR 973333
Phone: 541-757-7321

The Hanson Country Inn
795 SW Hanson Street
Corvallis, OR 97333
Phone: 541-752-2919
A short walk to the Oregon State University campus.

Country Bed & Breakfast
15840 W. Ellendale Road
Dallas, OR 97338
Phone: 503-623-6402

Woodridge Haven Bed & Breakfast
1830 Woodridge Court SW
Dallas, OR 97338
Phone: 503-623-6924

Places to Eat

Yaquina Bay Restaurant
325 Airport Road NE
Albany, OR
541-967-8420

McGrath's Fish House
Corner of Circle Blvd. and Highway 99
Corvallis, OR
Phone: 541-752-3474

Try the house special—parmesan cheese halibut.

Magenta
1425 NW Monroe Street
Corvallis, OR
Phone: 541-758-3494

Old Europe Inn
3195 Liberty Road S.
Salem, OR 97301
Phone: 503-588-3639

Morton's Bistro NW
1128 Edgewater
Salem, OR
Phone: 503-585-1113
Web site: www.mortonsbistronw.com

DaVinci Ristorante
180 High Street SE
Salem, OR 97301
Phone: 503-399-1413

Change of Seasons Restaurant
300 Liberty SE
Salem, OR
Phone: 503-365-9722

Things to Do

RD Steeves Imports
140 W. Main-Highway 47
Yamhill, OR 97148
Phone: 503-662-3999
Antiques at great prices.

Spirit Mountain Casino
Highway 18 P.O. Box 39
Grand Ronde, OR 97347
Phone: 503-879-2350
Toll Free: 800-760-7977
Slots, blackjack, poker, craps, roulette, bingo and keno—all the big games!

Salem's Riverfront Park
West of Front Street (downtown)
Phone: 503-588-6261
Toll Free: 800-874-7012
Have a picnic, play games, enjoy a concert or other event.

Cooley's Gardens, Inc.
11553 Silverton Road N.E.
Silverton, OR 97381
Phone: 503-873-5463
Come see the world's largest Iris grower! Enjoy 200 acres of beautiful blooms—free of charge.